BOOKED TO THE MAX!

30 DAYS AND 30 WAYS TO INCREASE BOOK SALES

Copyright © 2019 by Shannon Whittington

All rights reserved. No part of this book may be used or reproduced in any manner whatsoever without written permission of the author.

Published by CLC Publishing, LLC.
Mustang, OK 73064

Printed in the United States of America

Book Design by Shannon Whittington
Cover Design by

ISBN: 9781091656123

Non-Fiction/Marketing

Introduction

I'm so proud of you for taking charge of your book's success and stepping out of your comfort zone to make things happen for yourself! These next 30 days will be fun and challenging!

So, how is this crazy challenge going to work?

If you haven't already, please join our author community at the Brainstorming to Book Sales Facebook group. It is within the group that you will find accountability and support throughout the challenge.

Within this book, I will share 30 different ways you can market your book and maximize your sales. You can do one each day or spread it out. The purpose, however, is to increase your sales, and to get that boost going, you must be consistently working. There will be some days that you may not be able to complete the entire challenge, but the steps should be taken to progress through the challenge step.

If accountability helps you, then by all means, visit our Facebook group and let us know how you're doing each day! Share your successes as well as your challenges. Being a successful author does not have to be a lonely journey!

There may be some days that feel remedial to you but remember - not everyone is in the same place and I've put this book together for authors in all stages of the journey. There is nothing wasteful, so if you already know what to do, do it anyway!

What gives me the authority to help you market your book? I have helped upwards of 150 authors become published. I've watched them struggle to get their books selling. Those who take my advice have much better success!

To date, I have published two other books for my non-profit Books By Vets. "Walk with Warriors" and "Resilient Warriors". We are currently working on our third, "Red Dirt Vets".

I have been featured on multiple podcasts, have been asked to speak to many groups and have attended a conference in San Antonio, TX as a speaker. I have been a guest on radio shows numerous times and have appeared on our local ABC affiliate morning news show multiple times.

I don't just teach this stuff – I do it!

One last thing before we get started: I am always here if you have a question! If you do not feel comfortable posting a question in the Facebook group, feel free to email me directly. Send your email questions to: braintormingtobooksales@gmail.com. I WANT this to be a success for you!!! Don't give up in frustration or confusion. You have help - use it!!

Now - on to Day 1…

DAY #1

Who should read your book?

If you are a client of mine, you may have already completed this exercise. I feel this is such an integral exercise for becoming a successful author.

Define your WHO. Who is your book for? Who will read it? Who did you write it for? Who will buy it? Where is this person? Where do they hang out? What is their occupation? How old is this person? What do they do for fun? Did this person graduate high school? College?

There may be multiple answers to these questions. That's ok! As you're working through this, go deep. The purpose of this activity is to know where and how to market your book.

If you want a little added fun, you can even give your person a name.

Knowing who you have written your book for, down to details, will help you to better position your marketing.

DAY #2

Why did you write your book?

Now that you have determined just *who* your book is for, it's time to really understand WHY you want your book read. This may seem tedious to some of you. Stay with me...

When you understand WHY someone wants to read your book, or why they *need* to read it, or even why YOU want or need them to read it, it becomes easier for you to market your book. You will sound more confident when contacting people about buying or marketing your book.

If I were to say to you, "Read this book - it's awesome", is that going to be enough to convince you to invest hours or your time reading the book? Unless we REALLY know one another and you already trust that I understand what you enjoy and what you would gain from reading the book, chances are high that you'll give me a polite "I'll look into it" and never actually pick that book up.

However, if I can tell you exactly WHY I feel the book would be good for you, your group, your business, your family, etc., then your interest may be piqued just enough to take a look at the book.

Need ideas?

They will learn (fill in the blank)
They will be helped (in what area?)
They will be entertained
They will grow in (fill in the blank)
They will need my services in (fill in the blank)

The list could go on and on, but I think you get the idea!

Even if you have not yet finished writing your book, DO THIS EXERCISE! It will help you in the long run!

DAY #3
Where Are They?

You know how WHO your book is for (who's buying it) and WHY... Now, where do you find these people??

That's the million-dollar question, right?

There are many places you may find your readers.

Questions to ask yourself:

What do they enjoy?
What help do they need, and where are they looking for it?
What places do they visit frequently?
What groups might they be part of?
Where do they spend their time online?

If *you* were *them*, where would you expect to find a book like yours?

I could go on and on with a list of questions, but I don't want to overwhelm you. Brainstorm and come up with your Top 5 "Wheres". Keep this list handy. You will use it to schedule events, locate them on Facebook, target Facebook ads, etc.

DAY #4
Your Author Facebook Page

You've tackled the basics - defining WHO you're writing for, WHY they want to read your book, and WHERE to find them. Now, let's go get them!

You most likely already have a personal Facebook page. You may even be talking about your book on your page. That's GREAT! Now, you need an Author page on Facebook.

Being an author is a business and it needs to be treated as such. So, for today, I want you to set up your author Facebook page. This shouldn't take but maybe 15 minutes of your time.

From your personal page, you will be able to Create A Page. In naming your page, give it YOUR name - Author. (ex. Shannon Whittington - Author). Do not name it the name of your book. The exception to this would be if you have a business that your book was written for and you already have a business page where you can market your book.

Your profile picture should be one of you. It should be relatable. A picture of you at a book signing or event, if you already have one. A picture of you with your book. A picture of you with family. Or just a nice picture of yourself. Keep it professional – this is your business.

Your cover photo can be of your book cover (or a compilation of all your books if you have more than one!), a cover photo generated with your book title, a favorite quote from your book, the date of your upcoming release... If you're currently writing, putting the release date on the cover photo can be powerful for not only your readers, but for yourself as well!

There are many apps to create a cover photo. Canva.com is quite easy and can be used for free.

If your book is already published, be sure to include links to purchase the book on your page. Not as timeline posts, but rather in the "About" section of the page. You always want to make it as simple as possible for people to find your book and buy it.

Once your page is created, add a few posts to it. You'll use this page to talk about your book, post blogs that you write, share fun quotes from your book, talk about your journey to becoming an author, sharing your why, sharing events you'll be at with your book, etc. So, get a few posts on the page, then share your Author page to your Personal page, inviting people to "like" it.

Any time you make a post to your Author page, be sure to share it to your personal page. Don't be afraid to ask people to share for you, as well. This helps grow your reach and increase your visibility.

DAY #5

Facebook Groups

By now you should have a Facebook page for yourself as an author. Now let's talk about creating a Facebook GROUP.

What's the difference?

A page is where you simply share information. A group is where you build community.
Why do you need community as an author?

The people who join your Facebook group will be your biggest fans. Even if you have not yet released your book, you definitely want to build this group!

The people in your group will receive exclusive content from you. Sample chapters. Early release tickets to events you'll be at. First look at any upcoming books.

Most importantly, because of the community you build, they will become SUPER fans. They will share the content you post on your Page, they will voluntarily post about your book and speak to others, they will SHOW UP to your live events (book signings, etc.), they will gladly post reviews of your book on Amazon for you... the list goes on.

You create the GROUP from your PAGE. The two will be connected. To begin with, keep your group Closed - meaning, people must be approved to be added. This will help you guarantee you have "fans" in your group. While critics are appreciated and can help with growth, that's not what the group is for.

Once your group is created, make a post in the group thanking those who have joined. Thank them for being a super fan! Let them know you appreciate them. GUSH!!!

Then, post on your PERSONAL page, let people know about your group and ask if they would like to join. Post a link on your personal page so they can click and request. DO NOT add people without their permission!!! NO ONE likes that.

Often, when creating a group, it will ask for one member. You have my permission to add me. I'd be honored to be your Super Fan!

DAY #6

Extra on Facebook Groups

Yesterday I touched a bit on adding a Facebook group after setting up your Facebook page. You may be wondering exactly what a Group would do for you.

To put it simply, it's your VIP fan team!

What I want you to aim for, is to get 100 people in your group. Add me, and you've got your first! These 100 people are going to help you market your book. It'll be like having your own little marketing team.

Over the next two days, I will show you just how to work the group - so don't get too far ahead of me here!

For today, continue creating your group and inviting people to join. You can name this group after your book title. Use your book cover as the cover photo, etc. You could also make a cover photo that simply says VIP to remind people they are special to you.

Once the group is created, make a simple post that says something such as:

Thank you for being a super fan of my book! I wish to see my book in the hands of as many readers as possible, and clearly, I cannot do that alone. I have humbly asked for your assistance and am very thankful you have agreed! All I'll ask of you, is to share some posts about my book - which I'll even provide for you! Stay tuned for future posts and videos! As a member of this group, you will receive exclusive content, updates, etc. Again, THANK YOU!!!

This simple post will let members know you value them and welcome them all at the same time.

Whether or not you have already published your book, do this step!

Remember: the next two days I will show you exactly what to do with this group and how to work it!

DAY #7

Grow Your Facebook Group

By now you should have a Facebook page set up for you as an author, as well as a Facebook group for your VIP readers.

I've tasked you with getting 100 members in your group. So, just how do you do that?

1. Post a link to the group on your PERSONAL timeline, with a post about what you are looking for: People who are fans of YOU and your book.
2. ASK them to join to help you!
3. If you know of certain friends of family on your friends list who would be willing to help you out, send them a private message and ask them to help you.
4. When you post about your group, be sure to ASK people to share with others.
5. If you know of an author that you are a fan of, offer to swap help.

As you ask, let people know that you are asking for a 30-say commitment to help you with some easy marketing that will consist of simply *sharing* (they don't even have to come up with the content!) a Facebook post each day for 30 days.

Since you know what you will be asking of them, be sure you are choosing people who are on Facebook regularly and who have enough Facebook friends of their own to have an impact.

This will be an ongoing exercise – you most likely won't get to 100 members in a single day. However, you do want to get as many as you can, as quickly as you can.

NOTE: If you have not yet published your book, or do not yet have a release date, then you will continue building this group as you write. Interact with them along the way and begin the actual marketing 30 days prior to your book release. Don't wait to grow your group!

DAY #8

Group Interaction and Amazon Reviews

You have your group all set up, and hopefully you've started getting some members in the group who will help you marketing your book.
Now what do you do with all these people who are so eager to help you?

First and foremost, continue getting people added to your group. The more fans you have, the more marketing help you will receive. The results are truly exponential. For example, I share about your book; it resonates with 5 of my friends on Facebook; each of them share your book and it resonates with 5 of their friends, and so on. You can see how quickly the information starts getting out.

If you've already released your book, this process will help get the word out and allow you to gain more sales. If you have NOT yet released your book, this will help gear you up for a fantastic launch.

So - how do you work this?

EVERY DAY for 30 days you will post something in your group that is about you or your book. It can be a written post or a short video. What sort of things can you post?

- Quotes from the book
- Who you are trying to help with your book
- Character descriptions of some of your favorite characters in your book
- Cliff hangers
- Ideas for sequels
- Quotes of inspiration around the topic of your book
- Memes
- Stories about your writing process
- As the month goes on, you can ask the group questions

Get creative!

Remind your super fans that they then need to share your post to their personal page. That's all they have to do! The do not have to come up with their own content. Just copy and paste or click share. (At this point, consider making your group public so your super fans can share your content – especially if you are posting images or videos you want them to share. If it's text only, you can keep the group closed.)

You'll want to come up with a hashtag. It can be your book title (if it's not too long), it can be the release date... it needs to be something you'll remember, something recognizable, and rather short. ANYTIME you post about your book, or your fans post, this hashtag must be used!

Why a hashtag? Hashtags make your content searchable. You'll be able to easily find all posts about your book. A good hashtag will also help grow the visibility of your posts on platforms like Instagram. People search Instagram by hashtag - if your post shows up in their search, you may very well gain a new follower. At the very least, one new person - previously unknown to you - just learned about your book!

So, back to your posts: Ask your fans to post about your book, be sure to ask them to include your hashtag, as well as to tag you in the post. For the best response from your fans, give them exactly what you'd like them to post. Tell them. Type it so all they have to do is copy/paste. People want to help you! People are also impatient and lazy.

If your book has already released, and you have an Amazon link, I want you to post the link. In this post, ask for your fans to go to the link and post a review of your book. Now, understand this may not happen immediately. They probably ought to read it. A very easy way to get this to happen quickly, is to have a Kindle/E-book version of your book that you can give away to your fans or adjust the price to 99 cents for 30 days. This can be a huge thank you to them for helping you out.

If you have not yet released your book, let your fans know that eventually, you will be asking for this help. Let them know you will provide them with so much information about your book, as well as a 99 cent Kindle version as a thank you for their help.

Why 99 cents and not free? If all 100 people download your 99 cent Kindle book on release day, guess what happens? A very good chance that you hit best-seller is what happens! If being able to refer to yourself as a best-selling author is important to you, then you will absolutely want to work this program!

Amazon reviews are important! The more positive reviews you have, the higher on the search results within Amazon your book will be. The higher your book, the more organic reach you'll have for people to find your book when they are searching for what you have written.

If you have questions about this process, *please* let me know! Find me in the Brainstorming to Book Sales Facebook group, or email me at:

brainstormingtobooksales@gmail.com.

DAY #9

Facebook LIVE!

If the idea of doing live video terrifies you, you are not alone! If figuring it out for the first time and worrying about what everyone will think terrifies you, you are not alone! If going live and sharing your message excites you, you are not alone!

Now, before you simply close this email and say "Nope. Not me. Not gonna do this one!", I ask that you stay with me and at the very least, finish reading the chapter.

People connect and receive information in a few different ways: As an author, you can capitalize on *reading*, *hearing*, and *watching*.

Your written posts are going to be great and will reach many people. But not all of them. What about those that need to HEAR information before it really clicks for them? How do you reach them online?

Video.

If you think of a Facebook Live as nothing more than a conversation with friends, you will be great! If you've never done a live video before, I recommend keeping it very simple. Just do your video and worry about answering questions and replying to comments after you've finished. Once you're comfortable with the process and timing, you can graduate to responding to people as they post.

What should your LIVE be about? Well, your book! Just as with posting, talking about why you wrote the book, what the journey was like, what you hope will happen, who your favorite character is and why, who your least favorite character is and why, who you hope to help, any events you have coming up, any specials you are running, etc.

A Facebook live does not have to be long at all. Aim for at least 3-4 minutes, as this gives people time to notice you're on and to join you. If you have people interacting and you want to respond live, do it!

Housekeeping Tips:

- Make sure you look presentable.
- Check your background... what will your viewers see? Fix as needed.
- Turn your camera on and see that the lighting is decent. If it's too bright, you'll be washed out; too dark and they won't see you.
- Have the camera at eye level - if not a little higher. Not super high - you want to look natural.
- If you're using your phone, have it positioned lengthwise (on its side).
- When you hit that Go Live button, count to 3 to yourself before speaking.
- SMILE!
- Work on your "ums" "so's" and "ands", but don't beat yourself up over them! The point is progress - not perfection!
- Look at the CAMERA as you speak - NOT at yourself (I learned this the hard way!)

Plan a Facebook Live once per week as you do your book promotion. You could do 2 in your group that are exclusively for them and 2 on your page for the general public. The ones you do on your author page should also be shared to your personal page!

Don't forget to use your hashtag when you share your video.

How do you start a Facebook live?

- Go to your author Facebook Page.
- Go to where you would typically make a Post.
- Just above where you would normally type your post, you will see the word "Live". Click it.
- When the camera comes on, check how you appear, your background, lighting, etc.
- To the right of your face, you will see an area to choose where to broadcast. Choose Your Page or Group.
- Below that, you will see a place to type something about the video. Type a short blurb about what you'll be talking about.
- Add tags if you'd like...this could be your book title, etc.
- Take a deep breath, smile and click "Go Live".

That's it!!

When you are finished with your live, there will be a button to push to end. Facebook will then work on producing the video to your page for you. You're done!

You can do these from your phone - so you can literally do them anywhere! Just make sure there isn't a lot of background noise.

DAY #10
Instagram

Doing Facebook Lives can be a challenge for many people! Proud of you for stepping out of your comfort zone and getting it done! That's what so much of marketing is about - and it's what will set you up to be more successful.

Great job!!

Now, let's talk about Instagram. You can find my business Instagram at @creativelieteraryconsultants or my personal Instagram at @shannonwhittington2.

I invite you to follow me once you have your account set up. If you already have Instagram set up, then this will be super easy for you!

Instagram works from your phone/mobile device. Download the app to set up an account. Again, this should be about you as an author if you choose to separate it from your personal account. It's a pretty quick and simple process to set the account up.

What's the difference between Facebook and Instagram and why both?

Instagram is primarily visual. You will post pictures and memes. Any text you add will be fairly short, and you will utilize hashtags like crazy! Hashtags are how people will find you on Instagram as they search topics they are interested in.

You can even Google trending hashtags that are relevant to your book to get the best reach. When you search a hashtag, it will populate suggestions for you. There will be a number next to the word. That number represents how many times that hashtag is being used. Look to use the ones that are being used the most often.

Aside from my personal branding hashtag (#bookwithpurpose) I do not use a hashtag that isn't in at least the hundreds of thousands.

I was never a huge user of Instagram and am still building my following. What I CAN tell you is it WORKS!

When you post to Instagram, you will be asked if you want it to post to your Facebook page as well. I strongly recommend doing this. It saves you a step and it keeps your message consistent.

Have fun with it! If you're unsure of what to post, look around Instagram to get inspiration.

Once you have your account set up (this should only take about 10 minutes) post your Instagram handle on your Facebook page so people can start finding and following you! The more people you have following you, the better your chances for book sales.

DAY #11

Scheduling Social Media

Let's work on scheduling out some posts for your Facebook page.
While you may spend an hour or so on this process, it will save you time in the long-run.

Some people will schedule out a week, 2 weeks or even a month's worth of posts to their Facebook page.

When you are on your Author page, and you make a post, it will give you the option to "Schedule" it for a future date. This allows you to spend bulk time handling your social media. A "set it and forget it" process.

Housekeeping Tip: Use a spreadsheet, like Excel, or at the very least a notebook. As you get going, it can be easy to forget which days you've already scheduled.

As you schedule your posts, keep them varied. We've covered this previously, but it's just that important. It doesn't always have to be just about your book. Change it up a little bit!

- Pictures of you writing
- Pictures of you at events
- Pictures of you signing a book
- Pictures of your book
- Pictures of characters, settings, etc. related to your book
- Quotes about being an author
- Quotes by your characters
- Quotes from your book
- Statements about what it was like to write
- Quotes from your favorite authors
- Your feelings about your favorite/least favorite characters
- Testimonials from readers
- Results testimonials from clients who have learned what you share in your book
- Links to articles about your niche/genre/topic written by other people
- Links to resources you share in your book
- Reminders on where else to find you (FB group or page/Instagram) - do this once a month.

This is by NO means an exhaustive list, but it gets you going.

While you cannot yet schedule posts to Instagram without a paid service to do it for you, you CAN schedule posts to your Facebook author page *as well as* your Facebook group. Just remember to keep the content varied. Occasionally, post on your page reminding people about your group - keep that growing! As well as posting in your group reminding them to "like" your Facebook page and to follow you on Instagram. People need reminders!

Now, these scheduled posts are fantastic, and they guarantee you have content going out. Which you need! BUT - you still need to post organically as well. To mean, if something exciting is happening, post about it! You'll still need to be making posts to Instagram - share those to your Facebook page for "extra".

You should have a post scheduled to Facebook basically every other day.

***Don't forget! What posts to your Author page should be shared by you to your personal page! This lets your friends see what you have going on in the business world as well.

I hope you're inviting your Facebook friends to "like" your Facebook page and to follow you on Instagram. Do this about once per week. Do this from your Author page where it allows you to send invites.

I'm setting you free on your social media now! It's time to move on to other forms of marketing. Keep going with your posts and social media activity! Just because I'm no longer focusing on social media going forward doesn't mean you get to stop doing it.

DAY #12

Websites and Domain Names

I'm not going to lie - I hate websites.

Ok - maybe I don't hate actual websites but creating them and setting them up literally brought me to tears of frustration when I was first starting my business. However, it doesn't have to be that way. The problem I faced was I tried to WAY over-complicate the process. Just keep it simple and you will be ok!

You may be very tech savvy and have zero issues whipping up an awesome website in record time. Or, you may think you need a degree before you can set up your own website. If you're like me, you're somewhere in between.

What do you need to set up a website?
#1: A domain name. How do you do that? There are several websites that sell domain names. I personally use GoDaddy.com to purchase my domain names. When you purchase a domain, you will be offered a lot of other services

to add-on. While it's absolutely your choice to purchase those or not, really consider if you feel they're necessary.

#2. A host for your website. I do NOT recommend GoDaddy as the host of your website. Depending on your level of expertise, I recommend WordPress.org or an easy builder such as Wix.com.

Due to my LOW level of expertise, I have chosen to pay someone to create my website for me through WordPress.org. I have also used Wix.com for ease of use on other websites. Both will work just fine for your purposes as an author.

Purchasing a domain does not have to be expensive. No more than $15-$20. In choosing a domain name, keep it short and simple. You want it to fit nicely on marketing materials. You want it to be easy to understand and to fit your brand.

www.yourauthorname.com would be perfect!

Example: www.shannonwhittington.com or www.authorshannongwhittington.com

If you can get YOUR NAME, do it!!!

There are also different options for websites such as .com, .co, etc. Do your best to get a .com. People have been trained to type .com. While others are becoming more popular, my advice is to always make it as easy as possible for people to find you.

If you purchase a .co and someone else buys the same domain name but with a .com, people looking for you will often go to the .com in error. Just make it as easy as you can for people to find you! Why would someone opt for a .co website? They're less expensive by a couple dollars. That's it.

Once you have your domain name, you can then set up your website. Keep your website simple as well! One page is all that's really needed. What should be included?

- Your biography. Keep this short but hit on key points that people want to know and will help build your brand. This can be text with a picture of you, or it can be a video.
- Pictures of your book covers.

- Link to purchase your book or a "Coming Soon" statement
- Calendar to your events
- Links to your social media
- Links to your blog (we'll get to this soon!)
- A contact form (where people can give their name/email with a request to connect with you)
- A lead magnet (we'll get to this soon!)

That's it! Don't let the idea of setting up a website overwhelm you. Get help if you need it. If you don't know someone who can set a website up for you, let me know and I can connect you with my designer.

You can also check out www.fiverr.com and search for Website Design for low-cost options as well. Don't let fear stop you!

There are ways to get this done if website design is not in your wheelhouse or if you just don't feel like spending the time to do it. This is one step where it is absolutely ok to have it done for you.

Progress over perfection! Worry about getting the basics set up. You can get it "pretty" along the way. Setting up a website should take less than a day.

DAY #13

Lead Magnets

You may be asking "What exactly is a Lead Magnet"? Well, what does a magnet do? It attracts things. In this case, you will create a virtual magnet which will attract leads. If you've not been in sales/marketing before, you may be wondering what a lead is. A lead is someone who *may* want to purchase what you're selling. In your case, your book.

Essentially, the purpose of a lead magnet is to obtain the name and email address of someone interested in your book. Email addresses have become rather guarded by people in recent years due to loads of SPAM, so for someone to be willing to hand over their email address to you, you need to offer something of value to them in exchange.

A lead magnet can be something tangible, it can be a request, or it can be a promise.

As an author, depending on what your book is about, you may have a companion e-book that you could deliver in exchange for an email address. For example, if you're a chef, and you have a book coming out, maybe you have an e-book of your top 10 favorite recipes that you'll send in exchange for an email address.

You could simply ask that they sign up to receive your blog/updates/etc. (I'll cover blogs soon!).

If you do not yet have a book released, you could ask them to get on a list to be one of the FIRST to know of your book release.

There are other ideas, but these are some to get you started.

What does this look like on your website? You know when you visit a website and a box pops up asking for your email address? What they offer you in that pop-up is a lead magnet. The pop-up itself is often referred to as a "Lightbox" in website design.

If you don't like the idea of a pop-up, you can typically add the offer on the web page itself. Look into your website design to see how to do that, as different websites handle this differently. How you set this up will depend on what platform you used to build your website, so I'm not able to give those specific details here.

Why would an author need a lead magnet? To have a list of people who are already interested in you and your book to send notifications and updates to about: release dates, book signings, events, etc. These people will likely want to receive your blog as well!

DAY #14

Success Tracking

You've spent some time getting everything set up: social media accounts and websites. We're about to embark on some outside marketing.

You could "wing it" and just do what you feel like, when you feel like it, and hope for the best. OR, you could add a little method to your madness.

The best way I have found to do this is by creating a tracking system. But, what will you be tracking, exactly?

You will be tracking what works for you. This will let you know where to focus your efforts. While it's a great idea to try different marketing methods, what works for me may not work for you and vice versa. The easiest way to know if something is working is to track it.

Things to track:
- Social Media Platforms
- Website Traffic/Engagements

- Blogs read/engaged
- Book Signing Attendance/Sales
- Event Attendance/Sales
- Media Spots (radio/tv/podcast)
- Networking Event Success
- Book Sales
- Speaking Engagement Results

And any other marketing efforts you come up with.

Where do you track this information? I personally use Microsoft Excel. It's easy to sort and filter. Easy to adjust. I can keep it super simple or make it as fancy as I'd like. Google spreadsheets work much the same way.

While this may feel like a bit of extra work in the beginning, what it will ultimately do for you is simplify your work by showing you what marketing tactics work for you, and which don't.

You can find a very simple tracking sheet in the Files section of Brainstorming to Book Sales on Facebook. It will be an Excel spreadsheet. Take it and make it your own. Use it for inspiration to create something that works specifically for you if mine doesn't feel right to you.

The main take away from this is that you have some sort of tracking system in place so you can be sure your efforts are paying off and you're not wasting time doing things that just don't work for you.

Housekeeping Tip: This does NOT mean try it once, get frustrated with results, and never try again!! Tracking is a record of history...several attempts over time and looking for trends. Give all efforts at *least* a 3 month go to see if it's working for you or not.

Set your spreadsheet up and saved so you have easy access to it. I recommend saving on the cloud for easy access from any location/device and no fear of losing important information in the event of a computer crash or theft.

DAY #15

Let's Make a Deal!

Today you're going to come up with a special offer.

Special offers are a great way to raise awareness for your book and grow sales.

You can decide if your offer is going to include all versions of your book (Kindle/hardcopy/audio) or just one version. You decide if it's a lower price, or maybe free Kindle versions for a specific period of time.

You will want to post about your offer on your Facebook author page - then share it to your personal page. This *could* be your Live video for the week! Talk it up, be excited about it!

In your post, be sure to include ALL details!

- *Price*
- *Duration*
- *Version of the book (hardcopy, Kindle, etc.)*

- *WHY you're doing the offer*
- *Where they can buy it!!!!!*

You would be AMAZED at how many times people want to sell something and forget to tell buyers where to buy it! Post your link to Amazon or your website - wherever it is you want people to purchase your book.

The purpose of running a special is to get a larger volume of sales to happen at once. Not only does this put money in your pocket, it also boosts your visibility on Amazon - meaning it raises your book closer to the top of the list when people search for your kind of book.

If you choose to go Live, have a copy of your book in your hand to show during the video. If you do a standard post, include a photo of the cover or of you with your book. Images boost the visibility of your posts.

Make a post on Instagram as well and remember your hashtags! On Instagram, be sure to include the hashtag #specialoffer. It will help people find it. Don't forget the Amazon link in your Instagram post!

Keep it simple. Don't overthink the offer. This process shouldn't take more than 15 minutes total.

*** If your book is not yet published, go through this exercise and PLAN what your first offer will be once your book *is* published! It will make it that much easier once you get to that point.

DAY #16

Endorsements

You may be wondering why we're talking endorsements when, up to this point, it's been all about social media and websites. I'll tell you why...

Endorsements lend credibility. If you write a sci-fi story and you are able to get a respected individual from that community to read your book and write a few sentences about how they like it and why, what do you expect will happen?

What if, in addition to giving you those few sentences, this person also makes a mention of your book on their own social media profiles?

You see where we're going with this? The reach becomes exponential! You see, with effective marketing, you don't need EVERYONE to hear about your book. You need the RIGHT people to hear about your book.

So, how do you go about getting an endorsement?

You may already have a connection to someone you know would be perfect for this. Don't be shy - reach out and ask! People love being asked to be part of something they can help with. It makes them feel fantastic!

Assuming you do not already have a connection, you can reach out on social media. Ask something such as "Who is your favorite go-to when reading/learning about _____?" Let people give you names of those they trust in your arena.

Make direct contact through websites/email/social media accounts with those you would value an endorsement from.

Mail copies of your book to those you would appreciate an endorsement from with a handwritten card/letter requesting an endorsement.

Make no mistake - this could take a few, even several, attempts before you get what you are asking for. Don't give up!! Write out a list of those you would like to contact, then work on it. You can absolutely reach out to more than one person at a time. There's nothing wrong with multiple endorsements!

Aim high with this one. Unless your best friend, uncle or neighbor happens to be THE BEST endorser for your book - the one authority on your genre/subject - then they are not who we're talking about here.

Wrote a book on computer software? Contact Bill Gates. I'm THAT serious. You simply never know what may happen and the effect it will have on your book. Contact Oprah, Ellen, the President, a former President. Then work down from there on your list. If it scares you because the name sounds too big, then THAT is where I want you to start!

The very worst that can happen is you never hear back. The second worst thing that can happen is your ego gets a slight bruise. Bruises heal quickly!

The very BEST thing that can happen is you get the endorsement of your LIFE and your book goes further than you ever dreamed.

Now, what will you do with the endorsement once you have it? Post it on your website and social media for sure! If it makes sense now, you can release a second edition of your book with the endorsement included. Or, save it for a later date if you plan on doing a second edition later. But DEFINITELY share that endorsement!! Use it on marketing materials (flyers, press releases, banners, etc), social media, websites, etc.

Dream big with this one. Have FUN with it! Time to take off the fear blinders... it's gettin' real!

*** If your book is not yet published, go through this exercise and start getting endorsers lined up and excited about your book! This will also help to add that extra layer of "MUST. FINISH. BOOK." Let them know when you expect it to be finished, so they'll know when to expect to receive the manuscript from you.

DAY #17

Book Signings

Time to make Barnes & Noble, or your favorite local book store, your friend!

Scheduling a book signing is not nearly as difficult as it may sound. In some cases, it can take a simple phone call, in others you may need to make a visit or two. For the purposes of this task, I'm going to use Barnes & Noble as an example.

Often, when you do a book signing, the book store will purchase books for your book signing. Any that do not sell, they will display on their shelves. The benefit to you is you are not out-of-pocket money up front to do your book signing.

When you contact a store, simply state that you are an author and would like to schedule a book signing. Then ask who you should speak to. Book stores WANT people in their stores - unless your book clearly doesn't fit their business model. For example, if your book is filled with foul language and adult content, you probably would not contact a Christian book store to do a signing event. Know your audience.

Once you are in contact with the proper person, talk about how they operate a book signing. Have in mind a day/time you would like to do the signing but be flexible. Often, with new authors, the store will have a group signing event that they will invite you to. If at all possible, ACCEPT!

A group signing is not a slight to you! It is the store offering you an opportunity. Go to the group signing and kill it! You will then most likely be invited back for future solo signings.

The person you speak with will want the ISBN from your book so they can search it. Be sure you have this handy when you make the call.

You do not want to "oversell" your book. Be enthusiastic, give a brief synopsis of your book, be thankful for their time.

Are book stores the ONLY place you can have a book signing? Absolutely not!!

Remember when you went through the process of defining your Who and

Where? It's about to come in handy! Call different locales and discuss the possibility of doing a book signing event. The main difference between a book store and an on-site event, is with an on-site event you will more than likely need to purchase your own books to bring and sell.

One technique I have seen work very well for on-site book signings is to offer a percentage of PROFITS (not sales, but profits) back to the store or a non-profit of their choosing. By doing this, they will typically help market the event for you to increase attendance.

If you have to bring your own books, I recommend having no less than 50 on hand. If you have a decorative table covering, bring it. Any signage you've had made, bring it. While these things are NOT necessary, they bring a professional aesthetic appeal to your presence.

Pens. Bring pens!! Notice that is a plural word! The last thing you want is to run out of ink while working to sign copies of your book people have purchased just for the honor of having you sign it.

Talk to people who visit your table, as well as those who walk by. Be kind. Be open to answering questions about your book as well as yourself.

TAKE PICTURES!!! Take pictures of your table, have a picture taken of you at your table, of you signing a book for a fan, of you WITH a fan.... You get the idea. Post those pictures to your author Facebook page and share to your personal page. Share them to Instagram with your hashtag along with others such as #signgingday.

Do a Facebook check-in at the book store. Do a LIVE Facebook video. Include store employees, the manager, etc. Be as personable as you can and HAVE FUN!!!

*** If your book is not yet published, go through this exercise and PLAN where your first signing will be once your book *is* published! Make calls and ask about their process and what they will need once the time comes. Start building those relationships now. It will make it that much easier once you get to that point.

DAY #18

Non-Profit Partnerships

Y'all, this is one of my very favorites! Partnering with a non-profit to help not only your book, but a cause you believe in as well!

I'm going to share two different ways you can work with a non-profit to help boost sales and feel great about it.

First, choose a non-profit. This can be one that's simply near and dear to you, or it can be one that in one way or another connects to your book. If you wrote a book about overcoming addiction, maybe there is a recovery center you appreciate. If you've written children's books, maybe an organization that supports children in some way.

Once you have your non-profit chosen, you start making it known that a percentage of PROFITS will be donated to that organization. Tag the organization in your posts. Talk about them when talking about your books. You can even contact the organization and ask to speak with them about your book, what you wish to do with the proceeds and see if there is any way they could help to make your venture more successful. Since they are benefiting as well, many will offer some kind of help. These conversations can quickly lead to the second way I will talk about working with non-profits...

Second, work in tandem with a non-profit. You get them on board with you and do a collaborative marketing campaign. Your book goes on their website, their social media, etc. You get invited to speak to the organization and introduced to their partners. You, of course, are advertising the fact that you're all about them as well. It goes both ways, but in this manner, you receive much more cooperative efforts from the organization.

With local, smaller organizations, this tends to be a very easy process. Typically, one or two meetings for them to fully understand your mission and message, and to get the leaders of the organization on board as well.

The most important aspects of working with a non-profit are having clear expectations and follow through. Don't bail on giving them the agreed upon percentage of sales. And be *CLEAR* that the percentage is based on your **profits**, not overall sales. You should not end up out of money with these ventures.

Remember: Profit is what you have left after *all* expenses.

It's easy for some people to feel over-dedicated to a cause and end up giving everything away. I caution against this. Not because I don't want to see charities receive help - but because I don't want to see you fail! If you aren't making a profit for yourself, you will soon run out of the ability to continue.

These partnerships can be perpetual - meaning you work with one organization only, and there is no end date. OR, you can mix it up. There may be several you are interested in - go for it! Do 30- or 90-day partnerships, so you may help various organizations. This will also help with future media opportunities, which we will get into over the next couple days.

Start doing some research and find a handful of non-profit organizations you would like to help through your book. This thing you've done is going to have more reach and more power than you may have considered when you first got started.

*** If your book is not yet published, go through this exercise and start making connections with these organizations. Use it in your social media marketing - talking about them, sharing why they're important to you, etc. Then, once your book is done, you'll have more followers to connect with who will want to purchase your book simply because they wish to support the organization you are looking to help!

DAY #19

Let's Talk Radio

Radio is an excellent way to not only share about your book and any upcoming events or news; it's also an excellent way to work on speaking and conversation skills.

The first time I was on the radio, I was terrified, not going to lie. Then I realized no one can see me and the host is going to lead the entire program. That didn't take away ALL the jitters, but it certainly helped! I guess it was akin to being on stage and picturing everyone in their underwear... it took the bulk of the focus off me. I could imagine people in their cars with the radio on. Listening to the radio - but not actually looking at me.

My first radio spot was about home building, and a program we were working on in a small town that was trying to revitalize. I was in sales. I wasn't the actual builder. I didn't know details about how a home is built and I only had as much information as had been shared with me about this revitalization program. So why on earth was I the one on the radio?

Because I was passionate about this program! I loved what they were doing, and I wanted to be sure as many people as possible heard about it. I wanted those who could be helped by this program know it existed. I wanted to help this town.

How did it happen? How did I manage to get on the radio? I met someone who hosted a radio show and struck up a conversation about this town's project. We talked for a bit, and then it happened - I asked. I asked if she thought this was something that would be a fit for her show. We spoke a bit more about the purpose behind having the story on the radio, she said yes, we got it scheduled, we spoke briefly about the content of the show and how it would work, and I showed up!

It was about 10 minutes of actual on-air time and it was FUN!

Since then, I've been on the radio numerous times with different hosts, on different shows, and for different purposes. It's always so much fun, and great friendships are often born out of those shows.

Your challenge for today is to find a couple talk radio programs that you could reach out to and get a spot scheduled. Folks, this is easier than you are probably thinking! Keep in mind, these hosts talk for hours, nearly every day... they NEED content. They need guests. If you make *you, your book, your story, your message, your intent* - any of that - relevant to their show, then you *will* get a YES.

Here's another area where the non-profit partnership comes in handy! Use it in your attempt to gain media exposure. Let them know where a portion of your proceeds is going. Let them know why a particular organization holds meaning for you. Be prepared to speak about this on the show - it turns you and your book into a human-interest story.

Once you are booked for the show, remember to bring a copy of your book if you have one. Also, write down important information that you will want to be sure to share. Things such as where to buy your book or sign up for notification of its release, book signing dates/location, events you'll be at, your website and social media addresses/handles, your email address, etc.

Then just have a conversation and have fun!

Tip - Radio is NOT limited to your immediate area! Many radio shows take call-ins as well. They'll tell you which number to call at what day/time and they will put you on the air with the host. Don't allow "There are no shows in my area that are a fit" be an excuse!!

*** If your book is not yet published, go through this exercise anyway! You can get on shows to talk about your book and grow interest - especially if you are working with a non-profit. One more way to gain the interest of the organization - you'll be giving them additional free advertising. Be sure to share your email address and website for people to contact you and to sign up for information related to the release date of your book!

DAY #20

Podcasts

Podcasts are very similar to radio interviews.

You'll want to research several podcasts and reach out to those you feel match your message. Podcasters are *always* looking for people to have on their show!

A key difference is that on radio you will often be on anywhere from 10 mins to an hour, depending on the structure of the show and what all they have going on. You also have several commercial breaks during a radio show, the host will often have to make other announcements throughout the show, etc. Your actual conversation time becomes a bit limited. Radio is nearly always live.

On podcasts, it's typically just you and the host talking for 45 minutes to an hour, no commercial breaks.

A couple things you will want to ask the host prior to doing a show:

- Is it live or recorded?
- Will you get a link of the show?
- Do they have a Q&A format (where they send questions to you ahead of time to prepare) or is it a free-flow conversation?
- Where do they post their podcast (iTunes, Spotify, etc.)?
- If you are someone who tends to use more adult language, ask about this - some are very strict about language, some are very open - make sure it's a fit for you.

If you struggle with the research aspect of this, or simply feel you don't have the time to search for podcasts, consider hiring someone to do the research for you. Sites like Fiverr, Upwork and others have freelance contractors who will do this work for you at a very low cost (I'm talking $5-$20). Some will even make first contact for you and you then simply need to make final contact to schedule the actual interview. No excuses!

Remember - it's just a conversation about your book, your goals, your mission, your non-profit partners, your journey as an author... all stuff you already know better than anyone else!

*** If your book is not yet published, go through this exercise anyway! Make those contacts. Start interviewing and talking NOW. Begin building your audience NOW. It will boost sales at release, it will keep you accountable to get that book done. It'll give you lots of practice for down the road. Don't wait!

DAY #21

Marketing Calendar

Trying to remember what you need to do, and when to do it, while creating new habits can be rough. Therefore, I recommend having a marketing calendar.

I'm going to share my calendar template with you. Open it, save it to your files, use it! You can customize it as you see fit. Remember: A calendar is only as good as the person using it.

By scheduling your marketing, you can see exactly what needs to be done and when. This should help you to see that there's really *not* THAT much time invested into doing your marketing. It just needs to be consistent. A lot of marketing can be done ahead of time and scheduled to post at a later date. Facebook allows this to be done within their site. Instagram does not.

However, there are programs out there that will handle social media scheduling for you. HootSuite is one option.

Many people will take one day a month to plan out and schedule that month's social media content. I'm a big fan of this practice because let's face it - life happens and it can get easy to forget to make a post or send out that blog. By getting it done ahead of time and using your calendar to schedule when something posts or goes out, you free up the rest of the month for in-person events, media, etc.

Now, just because your social media is pre-scheduled doesn't mean you don't add in fun stuff throughout the month! If you're at an event, snap a pic and share it to social media. On TV? Share that link to your social media! On the radio? Take a studio pic and post a link to the recording. You get the idea.

The calendar is a very useful tool to help you stay on top of your marketing. In the template I'm sharing with you, I have inserted some activities already. For the activities not already in the calendar, I recommend scheduling them as follows:

- Radio/Podcast: At least one per month
- TV: At least one per quarter
- Book Signing: One per month

- Events: Attend an event where you can sell books at least twice per year; Attend local networking events that make sense as often as possible.

Here is the link to get the template:
https://drive.google.com/open?id=1IfZKfebHILOMJC2wQBCUh33G1-EwbI4e

*** If your book is not yet published, go through this exercise and fill in what you CAN be doing with marketing now. Then, once your book is released, begin updating your calendar with other marketing that you will be doing.

DAY #22

TV Personalities

It's TV time!!

Depending on what you have written, you may feel as though there is no place for you and your book on TV. I'm here to tell you - You Are Wrong. Stay with me...

Remember the non-profit you are going to partner with? That's leverage for you to get on TV. Remember your WHY? That's leverage for you to get on TV. Is there an event coming up that surrounds your niche? That's leverage for you to get on TV. See where I'm going?

Just how do you get on TV? YOU ASK!!! It's really that simple. I have been on the news several times. The first was me sharing my story of being denied by an adoption agency to adopt a baby. The next several times were about my non-profit, Books By Vets, and books we were doing, the launch of our non-profit, and book launches.

The secret was making it about anything but me. It was about veterans. It was about unfair practices by adoption agencies that the public needed to be made aware of. It was not about me.

Google your local news stations. Find their "in your corner" type spots. Get an email address. Send a short email about why you would like to be on their show. If you can reference other shows they have done that have piqued your interest, do that. Let them know WHY you would like to be on their show.

HINT: To sell books is NOT a reason!! It may be your underlying reason, but it is not what you tell the news station. You give them your deep why. Your human interest why. Your "how I help others" why, or what you want to share/teach/etc.

When you are given the day/time that they're going to bring you on, be prepared. Much like with radio, you want to be sure you have your bullet points ready. It goes FAST on TV. Typically, you'll have less than 10 minutes and the anchor or person interviewing you will do a lot of talking. Write down your name, book title, event date/time if applicable, non-profit you're partnering with, etc. and have that ready to give to the person interviewing you. Make their job easier, while making sure they get things like your name and book title correct.

In your email, attach a picture of your book cover if you have it. They will show it on air. Dress appropriately. Be comfortable, but clean. Have your hair and make-up done ahead of time. Be prepared to be at the studio for at least 30 minutes. They will typically have you arrive well before air time and have you wait until they're ready.

Wear clothes that are easy to mic. The mic will attach to your back on your clothes, and run up your back to clip on the front of your shirt/dress/jacket/etc. You don't want to wear clothes that make this difficult, or clothes that are going to fall forward/down once the mic is clipped on.

While on air, you will be having a conversation with the person interviewing you. Make eye contact with them. You don't even have to look at the camera if you don't want to. Just speak to the person next to you.

After your time on camera is complete, be sure to ask for a picture to be taken in the studio with the person who interviewed you. Put this on social media!

Once your segment is on the station's website, grab the link and share it to social media! Let people see what you are doing! This is how you build a following. Make sure your non-profit partner gets that link as well, so they can see the work you are doing.

I know this will be one of the most difficult for some of you. Do it anyway. I am one of the most introverted and shy people you will ever meet. I survived it. You will too!

TIP: You will be ignored, and you will be told "not now". Keep at it! You will eventually get your shot! That time I ended up getting interviewed about the adoption agency? I literally emailed every single news station in Oklahoma. I emailed Dr. Phil and Oprah. I only heard back from ONE station. Just one. It was all I needed. I'm still great friends with the anchor who interviewed me. She has helped me on numerous occasions with other interviews. It works!!

*** If your book is not yet published, go through this exercise and start making connections! Start talking to people and building those relationships. Offer to bring a representative from your non-profit partnership on air with you to talk about why you have chosen them and let them talk about their organization.

DAY #23

Blogging

Blogs are a great way to communicate with your fans. It's nothing more than a way to share information.

There is a book called "Blog A Week" by Tim Priebe that I highly recommend to help you come up with blog topics if you find yourself stuck.

I personally recommend blogging twice a month. It's manageable and you are less likely to run out of material. That said, I know people who blog each and every week. Some even twice per week. The frequency really depends on you, the material you have, the time and dedication you have, etc.

Where do you blog? If you have your website set up, that's where I would recommend it! You place your blog on your website and share it to social media from there. If your website is not up and running, google different blog sites, or use a mail service such as MailChimp to create your content and share it to social media.

At the end of a blog, be sure to include a link to purchase your book, or to sign up to receive notification upon the release of your book.

Blogs are an excellent way for people to get to know you. To get an inside look into the author behind the story. You can share all sorts of fun information in your blog!

- Your back story.
- What it was like writing your story.
- Characters (if you have several characters, you could write several blogs!)
- Your mission. What it's like to be an author.
- What your family thinks about you being an author.
- Ideas from your book.

I could go on and on about ideas to blog on. Have fun with it and let people in! Connect. That's the main purpose of your blog.

Depending on what your book is about and what your purpose is for your book, you may also be able to re-purpose your blog posts. One example would be to compile several related posts into an e-book that you can give away or sell.

If you're having trouble coming up with a post for social media, you can always pull out a snippet from a blog post and turn it into a social media post. Don't be afraid to re-purpose content! It saves you time and can also make your message consistent.

If you know you're not going to have time to blog, don't be shy about looking for a guest blogger. This is someone who writes a blog of their own, but you share it on your website and social media. When this happens, you also get the opportunity to guest blog on their site. This is important because it puts you in front of a whole new audience and allows you to further build your own audience.

As you can see, blogging can prove to be very lucrative!

DAY #24

Talk About It!

Sometimes the simplest of things can become the most difficult.

When was the last time you TOLD someone about your book? As in, actually spoke words. Not a social media post. Not a blog post. But had an actual conversation and talked about your book.

It's time you started doing just that. Only one rule: It must be someone you have not yet discussed your book with.

You know when someone asks: How are things? What have you been up to? What's going on? What's new? What do you do? That's your opening to talk about your book!!!

- Things are great! Did you know I published a book?
- Glad you asked - I've actually been having a ton of fun getting my book published!

- There's been quite a bit going on - finished my book, got it published and it's now available on Amazon!
- What's new? Well, I'm a published author!
- I'm an author.

Your old habits are going to creep in. You'll want to talk about family, kids, your job. Stop that! Well, I mean, you can talk about that if you want, but LEAD with your book. Be proud! Let them know where they can get it. Talk about why you wrote it. Share info about your non-profit partnership. Add that emotional nugget to the conversation that grows their curiosity.

Just one person. If you build this habit, you will be AMAZED at the opportunities that find their way to you. Book sales, sure, but also much more than that! Speaking opportunities, media opportunities, invitations to events, requests for partnerships... All from a single conversation where you had the courage to share that you are an author.

Just talk to one NEW person about your book.

*** If your book is not yet published, go through this exercise anyway! Tell someone new that you are writing a book! Share your plans. Share your vision. You'll be surprised what happens!

DAY #25

Speaking Opportunities

Speaking in front of people is the #1 fear of most people. It doesn't have to be that way!

The best way to speak without fear is to have a friendly audience. A friendly audience is one who wants to hear what you have to say. They're already a fan of what you are doing, or what you are doing directly benefits them.

As an author, you have SO much to offer!

Think about your WHO from the beginning of this book. Where are they? Contact groups where they are and ask if they need of a speaker. Talk about your book and your vision.

If you wrote fiction, talk to writing groups, groups in your niche, or to the non-profit you partner with to talk about why you chose them.

Speaking doesn't have to be for a super long period of time. It can be 5-10 minutes, it can be for an hour. The great thing about being proactive is you can dictate what you speak about and for how long.

When looking for a place to speak, consider civic groups such as Rotary Clubs, Chamber of Commerce meetings, church groups, business groups, writing clubs, niche groups, etc.

A niche group is one that matches your book. If you wrote a fictional sci-fi book, seek out a group of sci-fi fans that get together and ask for the opportunity to speak to them about your book. If you wrote a how-to book for new real estate agents, start calling brokers to see if you can speak to their office.

When you speak, get paid!

Oftentimes, as a new author/speaker, you will not be paid directly just for speaking. However, you CAN sell books. The best way to do this is to offer to speak at no cost but request the host to purchase enough copies of the book to be given to each person in attendance as a gift to them. This way they are pre-ordered at a retail price and you earn the money prior to the event. Everyone in attendance is thankful for their gift!

You can also let the host know that you will speak at no cost, but you will require the ability to sell copies of your book onsite. After you finish speaking, you let the audience know you'll be available for a certain period of time for them to purchase a copy of your book - and that you'll sign it.

If you end up selling copies of your book at the speaking event, come prepared with change and a way to accept credit/debit card payments. Square is a portable and very easy way to accept card payments. It connects to your cell phone and money received it deposited directly into your bank account the next day. It's also free to get a Square device. Take pens with you to sign books!

If you are signing books, don't be afraid to increase the purchase price of your book.

When determining the price of your book at an event, make it an easy round number. $10, $20, etc. This makes it easier for people to buy it.

Don't overthink it. Don't over-analyze it. Just ask and get booked! Civic organizations and niche groups are excellent places to start.

DAY #26

Networking

As an author, you may not think networking events are all that important for you. Those are for business people, right?

Yep.

And guess what? You're a business person!

Being an author and selling books is a business. And people do business with people they know, like and trust. How are they going to get to know you if they never see you?

Now, I'm not suggesting you go to a networking event and sell copies of your book. What I am suggesting is going to networking events and meet people. Talk about your book, your message, your mission. Look to connect with people who need what you have to offer.

You may find people who could have you in to speak; who end up needing your book; who have an event to invite you to.

A quick way to find networking opportunities is to check out MeetUp for your area. You can also check with your local Chamber of Commerce, or even ask others what networking opportunities they recommend.

Networking comes in many flavors. GREAT opportunities exist that are no cost to attend. Even opportunities with a cost will typically allow you to visit once. If you take advantage of that opportunity, be sure to make the most of it! Shake as many hands as possible and share your story!

If you have copies of your book, keep them in your car. If someone asks for a copy, great!! Let them know you have some in your car. And yes, you accept debit/credit cards, because you have your Square payment device, too! Phew! Glad you remembered to keep that with you, too!

I'll be honest - networking is my least favorite marketing activity. I'm introverted, so walking up and just starting conversations with strangers goes against every natural fiber of my being. BUT - each and every time I muster up the energy and make it to an event, something wonderful comes out of it. Every. Single. Time. Moral of this short story? Even if it's not your favorite, do it anyway. Allow yourself to step outside your comfort zone and see what wonderful opportunities await you!

*** If your book is not yet published, go through this exercise anyway. Start making contacts!

DAY #27

Facebook Ads

Facebook Ads CAN be confusing - I'll try to lessen that confusion for you.

First, an ad must be ran from your Facebook Page - as in, your author page.

Ads must be mostly images, with very little text. Too much text will cause Facebook to reject your ad.

You have 100% control over how much you spend on an ad - you can run an ad for $5.

I won't go through every step to placing and running a Facebook Ad here. But I will share some tips.

Your ad can be for a number of things:

- To buy your book, visit your website (where they are invited to join your mailing list)
- To promote an event
- To promote your page...

Go to your Author page and you will see an option to Create an Ad. This is where you start.

As you build your audience for your ad, narrow it a bit. Don't make it for "anyone" in the "United States". You know who your target is - build your ad according to your WHO.

When you get to the Interest section of the ad, include things such as your genre, similar authors, key words for your niche. This is how Facebook will target who sees your ad. If you wrote a book aimed at moms, you probably don't want to target men.

Pay attention to the pricing of the ad. You can indicate the total amount you want to spend, as well as the number of days you want the ad to run. Facebook will run the numbers for you and tell you how many people they expect will see your ad each day based on your budget and length of the ad.

Try it out. Start with a small budget and just get used to the process.

Facebook operates on their own billing schedule, so the amount of your ad will not come out of your account until their billing cycle. This may not align with the end date of your ad. Keep this in mind, so you aren't surprised when the amount is deducted from your account.

Within the ad section of Facebook, you can also set a maximum budget. This is the amount you may never exceed when doing ads within Facebook. It's an extra layer of protection to make sure you do not accidentally over-spend.

Play around with it. Run a short ad. See how it does!

*** If your book is not yet published, go through this exercise as a way to grow the number of people who "like" your page. Get your audience growing!

DAY #28

Press Releases

Ah, the press release.

There are countless companies out there who will claim to send your press release to 100s or even 1000s of media outlets. A few of those companies may even be legit. For the most part, though, they are not.

Sure they may send out *something* about you and your book. But where are they sending it? Often to publications no one has ever heard of, or that have names that look like familiar publications.

To have a press release be effective, start local. Send it to your local newspaper - the large metropolitan paper, as well as your local small-town paper.

A press release is something used to inform the public of something. Something such as a local author releasing a book - or having a book signing - or a book launch event!

In your press release, you want to address the individual entity you're sending the release to. You want to share a LITTLE about yourself, and a lot about the book. A short synopsis of the book, your mission with the book, your non-profit partnership as well as any event you have coming up.

The purpose is to make it meaningful to those who will be reading it, to grow their interest in you and your book.

Be sure your contact information is included in the press release. This not only allows the media outlet to get in contact with you, but they will include it in the release so readers will have a way to contact you as well.

For the most part, you can create a single press release, then simply adapt the individual content as necessary based on who you are submitting it to.

For sample press releases, just search "press release samples for authors" in Google. There will be MANY to help get your creative juices flowing.

Press releases are great to send when you release a book, want to announce the release of your book, or you have an event coming up that you will be at.

DAY #29

Contest Time!

Contests are a fun and fantastic way to grow your social media following!

Create a contest where you ask people to "share" your page. Ask them to tag you when they share it so you can keep track of who has shared it. Put a deadline on the contest and let your friends know that at the end of the contest, you will randomly choose a winner from all who have shared it.

What they win is up to you! It could be a gift card, it could be professional services you offer - it could be a signed copy of your book!

This contest should be run from your personal page as well as your author page for the greatest reach. When you share the contest on your personal page, remember to paste the link to your page in your post! People are lazy - make it as easy as possible for them to share!

Another version of this is to again ask people to share your page, and that you will grant a prize to the 500th (or whatever number you choose) person to like your author page. I don't find these to be quite as successful, because what do the people sharing it have to gain? However, if this resonates with you, I would recommend incorporating something for those who share it as well.

The idea here is to grow the "likes" on your page in order to grow your audience.

DAY #30

Give Away!

Let's do a give-away. The give-away should be a signed copy of your book. You can get very creative with this or keep it very simple.

A simple give-away would be asking people to share the link to your book on their social media and choosing someone to give a copy of your book to.

Something a little more creative could be making a social media post and asking your friends to participate. Make it about your book - or books in general. Have people comment on your post and choose a winner randomly from those who comment.

This give-away is all about having fun and getting engagement in your post. This works well with Facebook algorithms to make you more visible.

Maybe you're struggling to think of a non-profit to partner with... create the give-away where you ask your friends to name their favorite charity and WHY - if you pick their charity, they'll get a free signed copy of your book.

Give-aways are an excellent way to increase engagement and get help. Have fun with it! Respond and engage with those who participate. It'll help encourage them to continue engaging with you.

Have fun with it!

You Did It!!

No matter how far you've gotten in this challenge, I'm proud of you! You've taken steps to become a successfully published author, and that's not something everyone can say. Be proud of yourself! Keep taking the steps necessary to get your book in the hands of as many readers as possible!

This book may be at its end, but your marketing is not! Use your calendar, continue using these emails, keep going!

The entire purpose of this book is to give you the means to make progress. It doesn't matter how your book is published (traditionally, self, or vanity), if you are a new, up and coming author, the marketing falls to YOU. Keep going. Become consistent. You WILL see your book sales increase!

You've got this and I am so proud of you for stepping out of your comfort zone and doing what is necessary to take control of your success!

If you would like to schedule a consult with me, reach out! Connect with me in our Brainstorming to Book Sales

Facebook group, or email me at brainstormingtobooksales@gmail.com.

Good luck!!

I look forward to seeing your success!!

~Keep Writing

Shannon Whittington

www.ingramcontent.com/pod-product-compliance
Lightning Source LLC
Chambersburg PA
CBHW021847170526
45157CB00007B/2980